PIANO / VOCAL / GUITAR

THE BEST OF
MARC COHN

Cover image © 2020 Kim Mancuso Photography

ISBN 978-1-70510-708-9

Visit Hal Leonard Online at
www.halleonard.com

Contact us:
Hal Leonard
7777 West Bluemound Road
Milwaukee, WI 53213
Email: info@halleonard.com

In Europe, contact:
Hal Leonard Europe Limited
42 Wigmore Street
Marylebone, London, W1U 2RN
Email: info@halleonardeurope.com

In Australia, contact:
Hal Leonard Australia Pty. Ltd.
4 Lentara Court
Cheltenham, Victoria, 3192 Australia
Email: info@halleonard.com.au

GHOST TRAIN

Words and Music by
MARC COHN

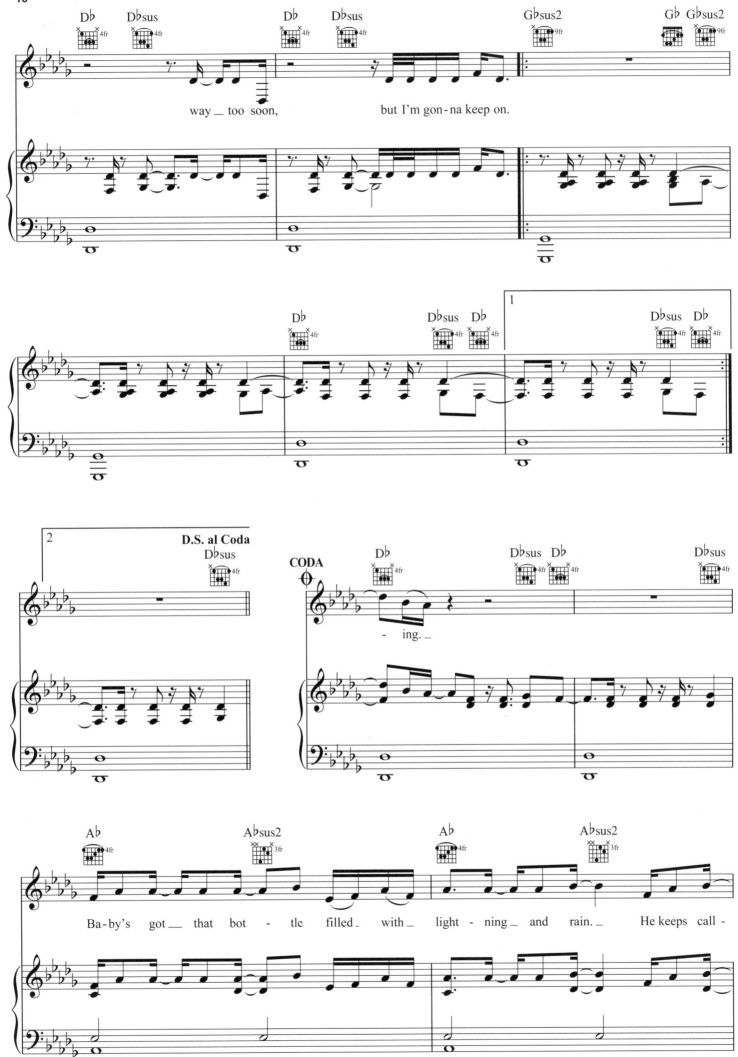

way __ too soon, but I'm gon-na keep on.

D.S. al Coda

CODA

- ing. __

Ba-by's got __ that bot - tle filled __ with __ light - ning __ and rain. __ He keeps call -

HEALING HANDS

Words and Music by
MARC COHN

LISTENING TO LEVON

Words and Music by
MARC COHN

Moderately slow, in 2

I was sit-ting with Mar - y in my dad's _ blue Val -

-iant. Rain was com - ing down and the

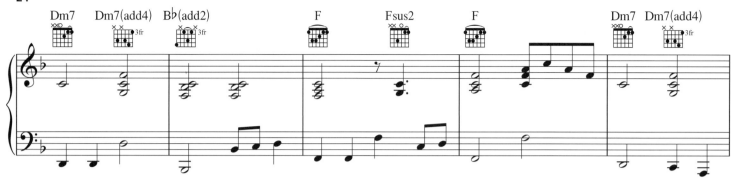

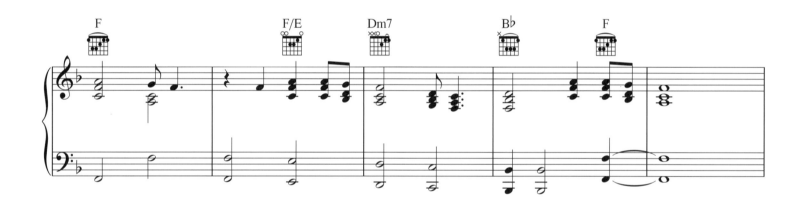

And it serves me right   if you can't e - ven hear me   sing - ing,

SILVER THUNDERBIRD

Words and Music by
MARC COHN

Watched it com-ing up Win — slow,__ down South __ Park Boul-e-vard.
He got up ev-er-y morn — ing __ while I ___ was still a-sleep,

D   **Em7**   **D/F#**   **G**

Yeah, it was look-ing good from tail to hood.
but I re- mem-ber the sound of him shuf- fling a- round.

C   **Bm7**

Great ___ big fins and paint - ed steel.   Man, it
Right ___ be - fore the crack ___ of dawn is when I

Am   **G**   **D**   **Em7**   **D/F#**

looked just like ___ the Bat - mo-bile.   With my old man ___ be - hind
heard him turn ___ the mo - tor on,   but when I got up ___ they were

G   **Em**   **D**   **C**

the wheel. ___   Well, you could hard-ly e-ven see him in all of that chrome, ___
gone. ___   Down ___ the road ___ in the rain and snow, ___
___ the road ___ in the rain and snow, ___

ONE SAFE PLACE

Words and Music by MARC COHN
and PHIL GALDSTON

yeah, _____ yeah.
yeah, _____ yeah? _
yeah, _____ yeah, _

Oh, life ____ is trial __ by fi - re,

D.S. al Coda

one safe place, ___ yeah, yeah, ___ yeah. ___

THE THINGS WE'VE HANDED DOWN

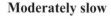

Words and Music by
MARC COHN

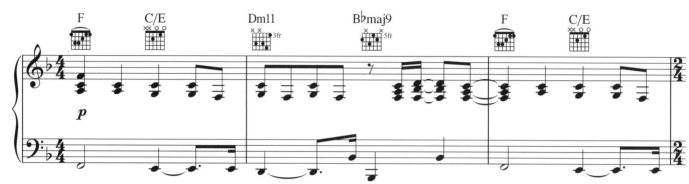

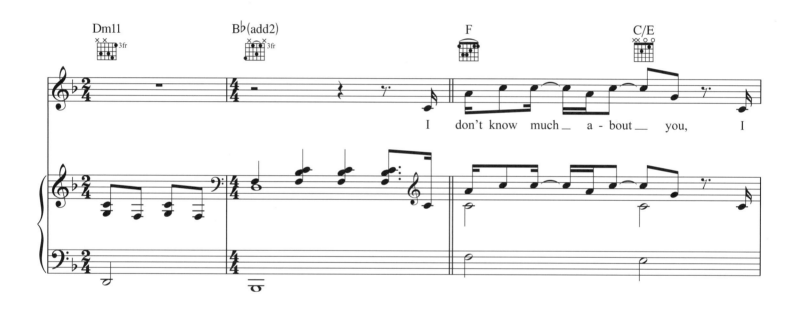

I don't know much _ a-bout _ you, I

don't know who _ you are. _ We've been do-ing fine _ with-out _ you, but we could

WALK THROUGH THE WORLD

Words and Music by MARC COHN
and JOHN B. LEVENTHAL

Walk through this world ___ with me. ___

I'm star-ing out a-cross the roof - tops, ba -

- by. I've seen ___ the writ - ing on the wall.

TRUE COMPANION

Words and Music by
MARC COHN

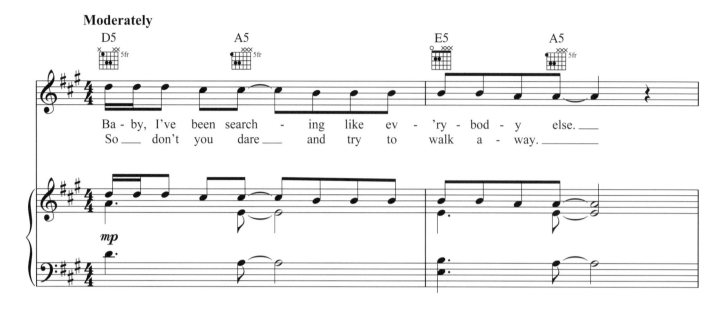

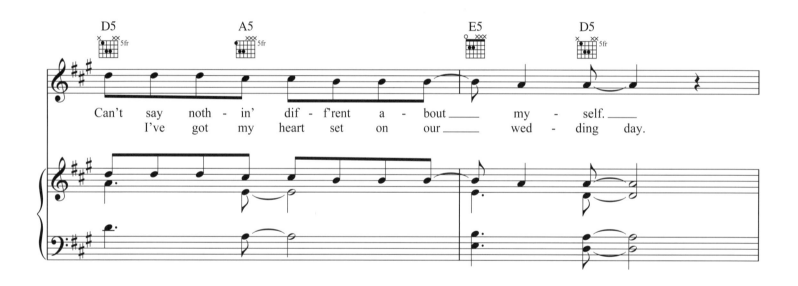

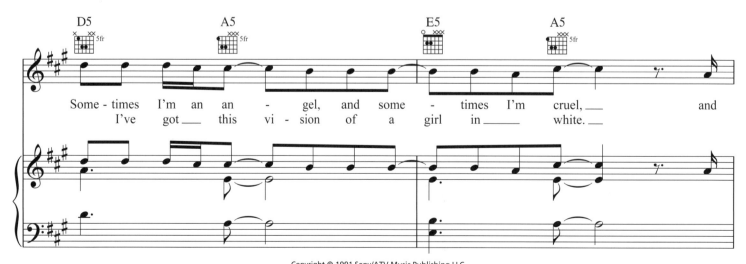

WALKING IN MEMPHIS

Words and Music by
MARC COHN

WORK TO DO

Words and Music by
MARC COHN

Moderately slow

A-round this time the

shad-ows _____ are tall, _____ when the moon's on _____ the rise _____ and the

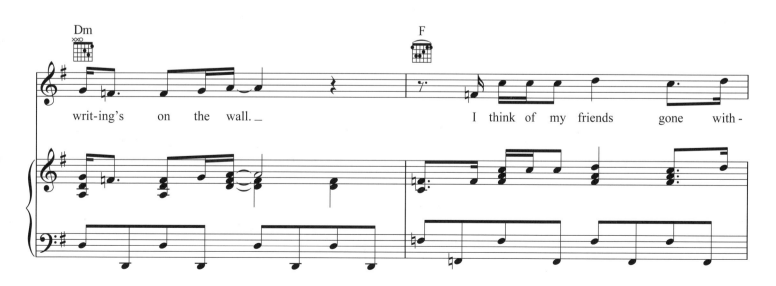

writ-ing's on the wall. _____ I think of my friends gone with-